Make Your Voice Matter With Lawmakers:

No Experience Necessary

BOSTON BAPTIST COLLEGE
LIBRARY
950 METROPOLITAN AVENUE
BOSTON,MA 02136
TEL (617) 364-3510 EXT 216

BOSTON BAPTIST COLLEGE
LIBRARY
950 METROPOLITAN AVENUE
BOSTON, MA 02136
TEL. (617) 364-3510 EXT. 216

MAKE YOUR VOICE MATTER
WITH LAWMAKERS
NO EXPERIENCE NECESSARY

Miriam Stein, MSW

ANOTHER LOOK
PUBLICATIONS

BOSTON BAPTIST COLLEGE
LIBRARY
950 METROPOLITAN AVENUE
BOSTON,MA 02136
TEL (617) 364-3510 EXT 216

Make Your Voice Matter With Lawmakers:
No Experience Necessary

Copyright © 2012 by Miriam Stein. All rights reserved.
Printed in the United States of America. No part of this book
may be used or reproduced in any manner whatsoever
without written permission except in the case of brief
quotations embodied in critical articles or reviews.

For information, contact Another Look Publications
anotherlookpublications@gmail.com

ISBN- 978-0-9849749-0-0

First Edition January 2012

BOSTON BAPTIST COLLEGE
LIBRARY
950 METROPOLITAN AVENUE
BOSTON 02136

"It is not incumbent upon you to complete the work, but neither are you at liberty to desist from it."

Rabbinic Saying from *Ethics of the Fathers*

Dedication

This book is dedicated to Violet M. Sieder, Ph.D. (1909-1988) an inspiring role model who taught me about advocacy and community organization, and about how to get things done.

Dr. Sieder's strong sense of social justice and commitment to action influenced legions of her students and colleagues. I feel privileged to have known her as a professional mentor and dear friend.

Contents

CHAPTER 6
Adapt Your Everyday Interpersonal Skills to Influence Lawmakers

- Register Your Opinion: Phone, Email, Write
- Build a Relationship With Your Lawmakers
- Get Acquainted With Your Lawmakers
- Understand Your Lawmakers
- Share Your Firsthand Experiences
- Stay Focused on Your Goals
- Express Appreciation to Your Lawmakers
- Express Disappointment to Your Lawmakers
- Describe Issues in Another Way
- Recognize and Acknowledge Mixed Feelings
- Form a Small Group of Like-minded People in Your Lawmaker's District

CHAPTER 7
Letters to the Editor and Social Media

- Why These Are Effective Communication Techniques
- Ways to Use Letters to the Editor and Social Media Posts
- Tips for Writing Letters to the Editor and Social Media Entries
- Effective Letters to the Editor: Examples

CHAPTER 8
The Extra Power of Specific Groups

- Volunteers
- Members of Religious Congregations
- Human Service Workers and Community Workers
- Mental Health Professionals
- Health Care Professionals
- Teachers and School Personnel
- Parents
- People Directly Affected, Their Friends, and Relatives
  - □ Low-income People □ People With Disabilities
  - □ Immigrants and Refugees

APPENDIX
Guide to Resources to Help You Advocate

INTRODUCTION

You Can Make a Difference
in 15 Minutes a Month

The frustration in the church parlor was palpable. The suburban congregants had volunteered for years cooking meals at soup kitchens, collecting winter coats for homeless families, and donating money to shelters. Still, they were overwhelmed that the needs kept growing. Some began to feel burned out.

At this monthly meeting of the church's social concerns committee they told me that they wanted to eliminate the root causes of family homelessness, not just put on band-aids.

As the advocacy consultant to Cooperative Metropolitan Ministries, an interfaith coalition that works for a just society, it was my job was to guide this group to understand that members could play a key role in reducing the root causes of family homelessness and poverty.

But first they had to believe that they could add legislative advocacy to their volunteer work in just a few minutes a month—no need to "quit their day job." All the congregants needed to do was contact their lawmakers a few times a year during deliberations on policies and funding for lifeline services such as homeless prevention services and training programs for jobs that paid a living wage.

Two Surprising Truths

Before these men and women would feel prepared to contact their lawmakers, they had to be convinced of two realities: that two or three calls or letters from constituents often draw a lawmaker's attention to an issue and that they already had most of the skills they needed—their interpersonal skills. With a few adjustments, they could easily adapt these "people skills" they used in daily life to influence public officials.

Twenty-five years ago, as a clinical social worker, I, too, was ignorant about the impact a few calls could have. Even if I had understood, I would not have phoned, worried about what to say to the "experts." Besides, why would a lawmaker want to hear from me?

When I landed a job with an advocacy organization, I had to learn fast how to communicate with lawmakers.

How I Overcame My Discomfort
in Phoning Lawmakers

During my third week as an advocate with the Massachusetts Human Services Coalition, Violet M. Sieder, a nationally respected community organizer, and my boss, handed me a list of 17 state house legislators. "Call each one," she said as she picked up a phone to make additional calls herself. "Tell them our organization urges them to vote for an annual clothing allowance for children on welfare. It's a high priority for us." I wasn't about to tell her that I had never phoned a lawmaker, spoken to one, or even seen one up close.

That morning, as I dialed the first legislator's number, the palm of my hand that cradled the phone was getting damp. "Please, please let him be out of the office," I pleaded silently. How could I ever call the other 16 representatives?

What if they asked me a lot of questions I couldn't answer? What if they disagreed and challenged me to defend my ideas? What if they asked me if there was enough tax money to pay for the clothing allowance? What if they demanded to know what programs should be cut to free up money for the clothing allowance? I didn't know any of the answers.

To my shock, the friendly sounding person who answered my call, who turned out to be the legislator's aide, said she would convey my message to the representative. She asked me to repeat the name of the organization on whose behalf I was phoning and ended by saying, "Thanks for calling."

My Story: Part I
How did I come to be in a position to have to phone lawmakers? Or even know that those calls were an

important strategy to support poor and other vulnerable people I had become a social worker to assist?

The story begins in 1963 during my first year at Boston University's School of Social Work. I chose social work because I wanted to help people. Without a clue about what that entailed, I enrolled in a master's degree program in counseling. My internship at Rhode Island Child Welfare Services began in late September. There, at age 22, I was assigned a case that deeply affected my thinking.

I'll never forget the Parker family, whose names have been changed to protect privacy. Three years before, 23-year-old Julie Parker had lost custody of her six-year-old son Stephen because of neglect. He was found alone several times in the apartment he and his mother shared.

Ms. Parker had told the child welfare worker that Stephen was always defying her, talking back to his teachers, and running off when he played outside. She explained that she couldn't care for him anymore and begged the worker to put him in a foster home.

I met Stephen when he was nine, a thin boy with tired brown eyes and straight brown hair. He had been living in the group home for over a year, after being unable to adjust to three foster homes in the past two and a half years. He was removed from the last one, a farmhouse, after he had stuck a pitchfork into a cow standing in the barn.

The staff at the group home reported that Stephen never smiled. He remained uncooperative and antagonistic toward everyone. Children avoided him. Staff members were running out of patience. Several times a week, Stephen would hide under his bed and cry for no apparent reason.

Stephen's mother had seen him only four times since he was six. I was assigned to establish a relationship with Stephen and encourage his mother, whose address was unknown, to become more involved with him. My supervisor explained that his mother might be the only person in his life who could offer any consistency.

After three months of spending an hour or two every week with Stephen, taking him for walks, for ice cream and letting him poke through and empty out my purse, he was starting to trust me. Through their relatives, I passed along a message to Ms. Parker to come to the agency to talk. When I finally met her, I was surprised how articulate she was, and how much she cared.

I began to understand why she pulled back from contact with Stephen. With new tears welling up in her brown eyes as soon as she wiped away the old ones and her hands trembling as she talked, she confided that she felt like a failure as a mother. Each time she saw Stephen her self-image plummeted.

While growing up, she had been abused and didn't know how to be a good parent. She worked on an assembly line and lived with an aunt who constantly reminded her of her shortcomings. She loved Stephen, she insisted, and wanted to be more of a mother to him.

I started weekly visits with her, too. We talked about her feelings, her strengths, and how she might put her life back together. Soon, she moved out of her aunt's house. Within a few months, she visited Stephen every other week and took him home for occasional weekends. Stephen became more cooperative, cried less, and even smiled sometimes.

"Why hadn't the social worker who had handled the case for the past three years helped the mother be more involved?" I asked my supervisor. Ms. Parker welcomed and seemed to thrive from my interest and concern.

My supervisor's answer, expressed with such sadness in her warm, blue eyes, gave me a glimpse of how "the system" affects services. The social worker was responsible for 40 to 50 families or "cases." Often cases required visits both to a mother and to her children living in foster homes, talks with the foster mother, and contact with the children's teachers. The social worker couldn't possibly see Ms. Parker weekly, no matter how much it might help Stephen.

I didn't know enough to ask, and my supervisor didn't tell me why social workers had overwhelming caseloads and how I could change that.

In May, my internship ended. Fortunately, my supervisor agreed to work with Ms. Parker rather than return the case to the regular social worker whose heavy caseload would make intensive contact impossible. And, we both knew how much Ms. Parker would continue to benefit from frequent contact.

For the next 13 years, I continued to work in clinical settings, always with lower-income people. I enjoyed contacts with my clients and could see that my interventions helped many of them. Still, I didn't know how to remedy a system rife with harmful service gaps and insufficiencies. These included inadequate welfare grants, little affordable housing, and too few mental health services. Other problems were long waiting lists for subsidized day care, children placed in foster care because their mothers were homeless, and elders moved to nursing homes due to a lack of homecare services.

I was so frustrated, I even considered leaving social work.

My Story: Part II

Then, in 1978, I fortunately found a job with the Massachusetts Human Services Coalition, a public education and advocacy group that promotes policies and laws to help people who are ill, impoverished, or disabled. One of my first assignments was the phone call to the legislator described above on page 3.

After several anxious months of being sure that none of the clinical skills I had struggled to develop for the past decade and a half had much relevance at the state house, I realized that just the opposite was true. Many of my skills were directly applicable to persuading and influencing lawmakers. To my relief, I discovered some specific, concrete abilities that other mental health clinicians and I had at our fingertips, ones that we could use to improve the service delivery systems that determined the quality of our clients' lives. We could become effective change agents just by transferring and adapting what we did every day with clients.

> *Later, I realized that the interpersonal skills everyone uses in daily life with colleagues, neighbors, friends, and relatives are also well suited, with a few adjustments, to inform and influence lawmakers.*

> *And, I was stunned to see the power that residents in a legislator's district could wield, if only they picked up a phone or a pen.*

Over the years it became clear to me that no matter how much direct service was given by professionals, volunteers, service consumers, and other community members, we needed a more adequate human services system, one that was true safety net.

Even if I had known that decisions affecting the human services system are largely crafted in state legislatures and in the U.S. Congress, it might not have helped much. The truth is—never in my wildest dreams did I think I'd be getting involved with "politics" when I became a clinical social worker.

The little I knew about politics came from reading the newspaper and watching TV. To a novice like me who had never come closer to her state lawmakers than seeing them march in parades, the world of politics seemed inaccessible.

Besides, what skills could I possibly have that might influence decisions in the halls of government?

This book reflects what I learned when I left clinical work and absorbed myself in legislative advocacy and media work, first with the Massachusetts Human Services Coalition, then with the Massachusetts Chapter of the National Association of Social Workers and the Massachusetts Immigrant and Refugee Advocacy Coalition.

For the past 15 years, I have run advocacy and media workshops, often titled "Make Your Voice Matter With Lawmakers." Much of the content is based on my personal experiences and observations. Workshop participants include congregants from many faiths, community volunteers, human services providers, mental health professionals, health care workers, and immigrant leaders.

Afterwards, participants report they feel empowered to take action. Many communicate with their lawmakers. Some are thrilled to see their letters to the editor published in their local weekly newspaper's print or online edition, or even in the major daily paper in their area.

This book is based on those workshops. The experiences of workshop attendees helped shape the stories in Chapter 5, which are composites of real-life and likely situations.

In an easy-to-read and user-friendly style, the material in this book demonstrates how decisions that affect nearly all services and policies, from poverty and educational issues to environmental concerns and climate change, are crafted by lawmakers in halls of power. In city halls, state capitols and in the U.S. Congress, all constituents can influence those decisions if they express their opinions.

As I stress in my workshops: It is 100% certain that decisions will be formulated in the halls of power. The only question is whether people from all walks of life will play a role in influencing those decisions.

> *As someone who started out thinking that she was not an activist and wasn't political, I now know that, "Not to be political is to be political too."*

CHAPTER 1

The Many Questions This Book Answers

Will Lawmakers Really Listen?

Why tell lawmakers what you think? Will they listen? Will they do anything about the injustices that so upset you? Is it worth your time to try? Besides, you know you don't have all the answers, or even many of them.

You're no expert on ending family homelessness, poverty, or designing services that improve life for people who are elderly, mentally ill, or have a physical or developmental disability. You are not an expert on climate change. You fear lawmakers will expect you to know the answers. You want to avoid the embarrassment of looking ignorant or naïve.

Why even read this book? Why even hope that, somehow, you can affect how laws are made or if lifeline services get sufficient funding? Why even fantasize that the root causes of problems can be eliminated? Why even consider that you alone, or with a few others, can accomplish that monumental task?

Because in the back of your mind, you suspect that life could be much better for many people in difficult situations, that we can save the environment. Maybe you know this instinctively. Maybe you've gleaned it from the hardships you've seen through volunteer work or through your job in a school, hospital, or community agency.

Maybe you've come to this conclusion through reading or prayer. Maybe it's been from living in poverty or with a disability. Maybe you are elderly and need services that have long waiting lists or aren't available at all. Or, maybe you know someone who struggles with these issues. "There must be a better way," you might have said to yourself.

Yes, there is another way. It's a look through a different lens, one that opens up a reality that isn't on the radar screen of most people. The view from this wider lens hones in on the root causes of many social problems. Those underlying causes can be paid attention to and fixed. Accomplishing this task requires adequate "political will."

Lawmakers whose votes often control how these root causes are addressed must be convinced that enough people in their district want things to change. As a reader of this book, you are one of these people. So are your neighbors, friends, relatives, and colleagues.

As shocking as it may seem, two or three phone calls, emails, or letters on a subject can convince a state lawmaker to move an issue toward the top of his agenda. On occasion, it takes just one person's contact, as difficult as that might be to believe.

That person could be you!

CHAPTER 2

Running into Roadblocks

*Why People Are Reluctant
to Take the Next Step*

Regardless of their income or educational level, people may believe that their voice doesn't matter in the halls of power. Yet, in communities all over the country, millions of adults and teens are eager to reduce or eliminate the root causes of social problems.

Some belong to religious congregations that encourage members to cook a meal at a shelter or collect clothing for kids who stay there. Some, on their own, bring canned vegetables to food pantries or supermarket collection boxes. Some help out at their children's or grandchildren's school.

Some serve on boards of directors of non-profit community agencies. Some teach adult literacy or assist immigrants to learn English. Some work in social service agencies or have relatives with a disability. Some have a disability themselves. Some are students in high school or college. Some live in poverty and have their hands full making ends meet.

And some don't do any of these things, but are concerned about people who are struggling, and would like to help in a permanent way.

But for a variety of reasons, many of these caring individuals don't take the important next step for lasting change, the one that has the potential to fix the underlying causes. They don't communicate their concerns to their elected representatives at the state capitol or in the U.S. Congress.

Fifteen barriers that people frequently experience or have to overcome to feel comfortable and competent to contact their lawmakers are listed in the chart on the next page.

Fifteen Common Barriers:

- *Those guys up at the state capitol don't care what I think.*
- *They only listen to folks with money or to other politicians.*
- *You can't trust any of them; they're all crooks.*
- *They know so much, why would they want to hear from me?*
- *They're so busy they wouldn't have time to talk with me.*
- *I'm just one person; I can't do much.*
- *It takes hundreds or thousands of phone calls or letters to make a difference.*
- *I'd like to call but I just don't know what to say.*
- *I wouldn't call or write unless I knew all the facts and figures about an issue, and it would take forever to research that.*
- *I barely earn enough to feed my kids; why would a state capitol hotshot listen to me?*
- *I never finished high school and don't use a lot of big words.*
- *I speak English with a heavy accent.*
- *I'm too busy.*
- *I'm not political.*
- *I'm not an activist.*

CHAPTER 3

The Untapped Power of the People

Two or Three Callers Can Draw Attention to an Issue

"I couldn't believe that Senator Fargo called me back. My husband answered the phone and almost fainted when the voice on the other end of the line said: 'This is Senator Susan Fargo. I am returning Ellen Lambert's call.'"

An Advocacy Workshop Attendee

Massachusetts State Senator Therese Murray, the chairman of the powerful Senate Committee on Ways and Means, was working hard to find a solution to closing a budget shortfall. A lobbyist suggested that the legislature raise the annual registration fee lobbyists pay since they use the building's lights, bathrooms, and hallways. "You should charge us more," the lobbyist said. Senator Murray took him up on his suggestion.

The Boston Globe, May 22, 2003

When I stopped by an experienced representative's state house office to discuss an issue, I heard her tell a caller that she planned to vote against a proposal to change the area codes in her district. After she hung up, she looked me in the eye and shrugged. "It didn't really matter to me. But now that I've received 10 calls opposed to the change, I'll vote against it."

Recognizing Your Power: The Enormous Importance of Constituents

Everyone reading this book is a constituent.

"I feel comfortable that I do an awful lot of work in my district to ensure the voters continue to send me back to the state house," one representative said in a newspaper article.

Everyone who lives in a lawmaker's district is a *constituent.* Some constituents are registered voters and vote in most elections. Others vote occasionally. Still others live in the district but aren't registered to vote because they think voting doesn't matter or they aren't U.S. citizens.

Lawmakers never forget that the next election is just around the corner and that they need to consider whether enough people in their district will vote for them. Think how you would look at things if you had to reapply for your job every two or four years.

No wonder lawmakers always pay attention to the sentiment in their district. No wonder they carefully read the local weekly newspapers, especially the Letters to the Editor section. No wonder they are so open to meeting with their constituents.

Constituents sometimes have personal connections with lawmakers or their families and friends. These connections can provide access to the lawmaker at social gatherings or community events. Conversations in informal settings offer excellent opportunities to convey information or opinions.

Even with no personal connections, lawmakers extend themselves to meet constituents at annual meetings of community groups, public events, and when campaigning for re-election.

Every vote counts. In some elections, only 20 percent of registered voters go to the polls, giving enormous power to those who do show up. Occasionally, elections are decided by a handful of votes. One Massachusetts representative who chaired the key Committee on Human Services and Elderly Affairs won re-election by just 16 votes.

Lawmakers need constituents to work on their re-election campaigns. They depend on volunteers to stuff envelopes and hold signs, as well as staff phone banks and help raise funds. Constituents who volunteer get noticed quickly and often gain instant access to the lawmaker.

No wonder then, that people who live in a lawmaker's district are one of the most important influences on them. Few constituents realize that they have such power to shape their lawmakers' opinions and votes.

> *One woman from an affluent Boston suburb asked the key question during a discussion about the power of constituents. "Why would a suburban lawmaker prioritize programs that help homeless families? We don't have any homeless families in our town."*
>
> *The answer: Because the lawmaker heard from constituents who want her to focus on programs that can end family homelessness.*

Massachusetts State Representative Lida Harkins says, *"When a constituent calls us, we're looking to know how you feel about an issue."* She notes that she receives sufficient information about topics from lobbyists, consultants, heads of organizations, and state house researchers. She looks to constituents for their perspectives, not for data.

Massachusetts State Senator Cheryl Jacques reinforces Harkins' thoughts. *"Remember the roles,"* she stresses. *"We work for you. You hired us. You gave us the job. You pay us. So why not say: 'Cheryl, I need you to look at this and I hope you'll give it your effort.'"*

How Many Calls, Letters, or Emails Does It Take to Get a Lawmaker to Notice?

At the State Capitol or at City Hall

As shocking as it seems, *one, two or three* calls, letters, or emails to a lawmaker at a state capitol or city hall draw attention to an issue. Six or seven make it seem like the issue is important to a significant number of people in the district. Most people are astonished when they learn how few contacts it takes.

This book focuses primarily on making your voice matter with lawmakers in state capitols. While many of the same principles apply in expressing your opinions to your congressional lawmakers, there are some differences.

In the Congress

Because our elected officials who serve in Congress represent more constituents than those at state capitols or city halls, and face additional pressures, a larger number of messages are necessary to make an impression.

Why Do So Few Contacts Make Such a Big Impression?

Lawmakers don't usually hear from their constituents. Highly publicized topics like taxes generate many calls. But many topics that affect low-income people, as well as education and the environment, receive little media attention. Consequently, few people even know that lawmakers are discussing these issues, or perhaps voting on them.

Besides, most constituents don't automatically think of contacting lawmakers when they are upset about an issue, even if they suspect the lawmaker might be able to help. Calling city hall, the state capitol, or the U.S. Congress isn't part of everyday life, like grocery shopping or doing laundry.

Why Lawmakers Want to Hear From Constituents

Constituents give lawmakers a sense of what some people (at least the ones who contact them) in their district think about issues. Lawmakers assume those constituents have friends, neighbors, co-workers, or fellow congregants who share their views.

Lawmakers are sometimes pressured by legislative leaders or colleagues to vote for something they don't want to support. They are more likely to be able to resist this pressure if they can emphasize that they have heard from constituents who agree with their position. Lawmakers can also counter that they are worried about how they will do in the next election if they go against voter sentiment. This argument is taken extremely seriously in all halls of power.

Key Role of Legislative Aides

Legislative aides are a lawmaker's extra eyes and ears. They present information about issues as well as constituents' opinions to their bosses. They also help constituents obtain services or benefits ranging from subsidized housing to counseling. If you speak with an aide, you can feel confident that your thoughts will be communicated to the lawmaker.

Locating and Contacting Your Lawmakers

On the state level, at the state capitol, everyone has at least one senator and one representative. They are up for re-election every two or four years, depending on the state where you live.

On the federal level, in Washington, D.C., each constituent is represented by three congressional lawmakers. One is a member of the U.S. House of Representatives, called a representative, who is up for re-election every two years. The others are senators who serve in the U.S. Senate. Every state has two senators in Congress whose six-year terms are staggered.

Lawmakers, the elected officials who craft laws, also serve in city and town halls, on school committees, in town meetings, and other public bodies. All make decisions about programs, policies, and funding levels that affect all constituents and the communities where they live.

To quickly learn the names of your state and federal lawmakers, and how to contact them, phone your city or town hall. Find the city or town hall number in your local phone book. If you have a computer, or can use one in your library, go to the computer's search engine. Enter the name of your community and state and the words "city/town."

For your Washington, D.C senators and representative, you can also go to http://www.contactingthecongress.org and enter your address. Click on the name for the person's home page.

CHAPTER 4

Lawmakers Are People Too

Influences on Lawmakers

When two of us met with the chairman of the House Ways and Means Committee at his state house office, the first thing he said was, "Glad you came in to see me. Not many people from my district come here." Then, he smiled and motioned us to sit down in the red leather armchairs in front of his desk.

As the Director of Governmental Affairs at the Massachusetts Chapter of the National Association of Social Workers, my goal was to convince this powerful leader, who was deliberating the state budget, to increase funds for mothers on public assistance. More funding would help families buy nutritious food and prevent homelessness.

I had invited a social worker who lived in the chairman's district to come to the meeting, and asked her to set up the appointment. I knew that only a constituent could get an appointment during this time of intense budget negotiations and deal making. Requests for a meeting from my colleagues in an advocacy coalition had been turned down.

The chairman, wearing a grey pinstriped suit and a red tie, his graying blond hair windblown, leaned back in his chair. "I just spent four hours at budget hearing. So many worthy causes need money and the state doesn't have enough to go around." He frowned and shook his head.

"But this morning, about 30 pre-schoolers from the Head Start Program down the street from my district office came in. They're all so cute. Most of them begged to sit on my lap," he continued. "They liked to roll the pencils on the desk, too," he said as his fingers reached for the three yellow pencils, demonstrating how the children had pushed them back and forth.

"I'll make sure to allocate enough funds to Head Start," he said with a grin, "that's a great program."

We expressed our appreciation that the chairman was planning to fully fund Head Start. Then we pointed out that many of the low-income pre-schoolers were likely to receive some public benefits and made a pitch for adequate funding for programs that helped families struggling with poverty.

The chairman said that our explanation made a lot of sense, although he didn't commit himself to adequate funding for any particular program. We were pleased that our visit called attention to the important role programs can play in the lives of low-income people.

During the meeting, we also learned that the chairman is affected by firsthand experience with people who benefit from social programs, something to keep in mind for future contacts.

An hour later, we visited the office of my state senator. A former college administrator, he wore a three-piece grey striped suit and a dark blue and white tie. I explained that we had come to ask for sufficient funding for adult basic education programs. I started to tell him about a very low-income woman whose life would be improved if she could enroll in a job training class to prepare her for a living wage job.

The senator leaned back in his chair, shook his head, then put up both his hands with their palms facing me, in a gesture that says "stop." "Just give me the statistics," he said, "I don't want to hear any case stories." I told him I would get him the statistics and followed up a few days later. Never again did I give him an example.

Remember that *lawmakers are people too*! Many of the things that influence constituents' thinking affect theirs too. Keeping this key concept in mind may help you overcome some of your discomfort and anxiety in deciding to get in touch with public officials.

Every lawmaker judges the importance of each factor on the lists below. How a lawmaker weighs and balances the items is a major challenge of his job.

Some of the factors that influence a lawmaker's opinions and votes are spelled out here. You may be able to come up with others.

The Two Most Important Influences on Lawmakers

Constituents and legislative leaders are the two most important influences on lawmakers. Other significant factors that play key roles are listed below.

Constituents

The power of constituents is explained in Chapter 3: *The Untapped Power of the People.*

Legislative Leadership

The legislative leadership (leaders in the halls of power) are opinion leaders. They hold positions like President of the Senate, Speaker of the House of Representatives, Majority Party Leaders, Minority Party Leaders. They appoint lawmakers to committees and to leadership positions within committees. They also appoint other leaders and may determine who gets the better office. A legislative leader, someone like the chairman of the House Committee on Ways and Means mentioned at the beginning of this chapter, often decides if a special project in a lawmaker's home district will get funded. Such funding wins a lawmaker points with constituents.

Other Key Factors That Influence Lawmakers

In the Community
- Constituents, the most important
- Members of advocacy groups, unions, and professional organizations
- Campaign contributors (large and small contributions, even $25, get noticed and can help gain ready access to the lawmaker)
- Human services agencies
- School systems
- Religious leaders

At the State Capitol
- Elected and appointed leaders in the legislature, the most important
- Representatives and Senators
- Lobbyists
- Legislative Aides
- Financial contributors
- Advocacy groups
- Unions
- Professional organizations
- State and federal laws

In the National Arena
- Political party leaders
- Members of Congress
- Lobbyists
- Legislative Aides
- Financial contributors
- Experts on issues

- The economy
- Federal laws

The Media
- Television (commercial, public broadcasting, local access cable)
- Radio
- Movies
- Newspapers (dailies and weeklies, print and online)
- Magazines (print and online)
- Newsletters (of organizations, hospitals, corporations, religious congregations)
- The Internet
- Social media (blogs, LinkedIn, Facebook, Twitter)

Facts and Figures
- Studies
- Surveys
- Think Tanks

Personal
- Friends
- Family
- Neighbors
- Colleagues in former jobs
- Individual and family experiences
- Personal values
- Economic self-interest

CHAPTER 5

Six Who Discovered Their Voice Could Matter With Lawmakers

Easier Than Anyone Would Have Guessed

This chapter features six stories that are composites of real-life and likely situations. The individuals in the scenarios desperately wanted to eliminate injustices but were reluctant to take action, or didn't know how to do it. The vignettes in this chapter show how they shared their concerns and opinions with their lawmakers and felt empowered by the experience.

In some cases, the lawmakers agreed with their views and promised to take action. In others, lawmakers indicated their willingness to consider the arguments but made no commitment. Boxes that appear close to the text identify techniques these people used to adapt their everyday interpersonal skills to influence lawmakers. These techniques are explained in detail in Chapter 6, *Adapt Your Everyday Interpersonal Skills to Influence Lawmakers.*

Ed and Ruth

A high school teacher and father of two teenage girls, Ed, age 43, loves gardening and bringing his suburban yard to life with roses, jonquils, and pansies. He and his lawyer wife Ruth, age 41, serve on their church's social concerns committee. Once a month, the group cooks a meal at a shelter for homeless families, just a 20-minute ride from Ed and Ruth's house. The volunteers are troubled by the many problems the families face and want to do more to prevent families from becoming homeless.

Ed and Ruth also hope their involvement will serve as an example to their daughters. They never imagined they could influence policies or laws that would prevent homelessness, never thought of themselves as "activists."

They just want to help homeless kids and their mothers in a more permanent way. Neither realizes that in less than 15 minutes a month, they can significantly influence the fate of homeless prevention programs under debate in their state capitol.

Ed and Ruth's Story

Late one Monday afternoon Ed and Ruth were peeling potatoes in the homeless shelter's kitchen. The executive director, Sue, stopped by to tell them how much she appreciated their help.

Ruth noticed that Sue was wearing a black pants suit today whereas she usually wore a sweater and slacks. "You're all dressed up," Ruth said, wondering whether to comment further on Sue's clothing. Perhaps she didn't want to share too much of herself with volunteers.

"I just came from a meeting at the state house," Sue said, taking a deep breath. "Some other shelter directors and I met with lawmakers. The legislature is starting to put together the state budget. We're worried that with the tight financial situation, money for our shelters might be cut. I don't think I could sleep at night if I ever had to turn away desperate families."

"How could they even think about making you turn away people?" Ed said, wrinkling his brow. Looking at his wife and casting the potato peeler aside, Ed said, "I wish there was something we could do to help."

Sue smiled and straightened up. She had been thinking about how she could involve volunteers and shelter residents in advocating for enough funds for the agency. When she raised this suggestion at a recent board of directors meeting, the group thought it was a great idea. In fact, several board members proposed that they themselves should be making a pitch to lawmakers. But, they stressed that none of them had ever spoken to a public official. They felt uncomfortable about it.

"There is another way to help the shelter besides working in the kitchen," Sue told Ed and Ruth. "I wonder if both of you would consider it." She went on to explain that the lawmakers said they wanted to hear from people who didn't have a financial stake in whether or not the shelter received enough funding, people whose jobs weren't dependent on the shelter's budget.

"That's us," Ruth said. "But," she continued in a hesitant voice, "we've never spoken to anyone at the state house. I'm pretty nervous about it."

"So am I," Ed added. "Neither of us has ever thought about contacting a lawmaker."

"That sounds a lot harder than peeling potatoes," Ruth said. "Will I get bombarded with questions I can't answer? Even though I'm a lawyer, I don't know anything about the state budget. I help families with estates and wills."

Ed chimed in, "I teach high school science."

Sue understood their trepidation and described her first encounter with a lawmaker. Five years ago, when she worked as case manager at the shelter, she and the former executive director, who was an old hand at this, met with several legislators. Surprisingly, and to her relief, the lawmakers didn't grill her. They just asked her why the shelter was important in giving families a place to stay and helping them get back on their feet.

Ruth smiled as she turned to Ed saying, "Guess we could do something like that. After all, I meet with people all the time to discuss important issues, and you stand before a classroom explaining complicated concepts to teenagers."

Sue assured them that she would accompany them to the meetings with lawmakers. She proposed they meet with the ones that she had just seen, with the senator and the representative from the district in which the shelter was located, and even more importantly, with the lawmakers in their own district. "Lawmakers always want to hear from their constituents," she said, "believe it or not."

On their drive home, Ruth and Ed wondered if they had gotten themselves in over their heads. "What Sue proposed sounded so easy and straightforward," Ed said. "Do you think it'll really be like that?"

Ever the optimist, Ruth replied: "There's only one way to tell. We have nothing to lose and the families who need shelter have so much to gain."

Three weeks later, as Ed was putting on his favorite blue tie and navy sport jacket for the meeting with Senator Morrison, the phone rang. It was Sue. She had suddenly come down with a stomach virus and couldn't possibly join him and Ruth at the 4:00 pm appointment. "Could you see yourselves going without me?" she asked. "If not, we could reschedule."

Ed decided he and Ruth could go alone. After all, they knew from firsthand experience how the shelter and its services helped children and families over a rough time in their lives. Sue had also told the shelter volunteers that many families would be able to avoid homelessness if they could tap into a fund to tide them over if they owed back rent or overdue payment for electricity bills.

At the Senator's Office

Ed and Ruth opened the brown wooden door to Senator Morrison's state house office, not knowing what to expect. As they walked to the receptionist's desk, they noticed that two walls were decorated with plaques featuring the senator's awards.

"We are Ed and Ruth Long and have an appointment with Senator Morrison," Ed said. He added something Sue had told them to be sure to mention: "We live in the senator's district." The receptionist's smile said it all.

Once seated on the blue plaid Victorian chairs inside the senator's private office, Ed and Ruth could tell that this would be a friendly meeting. "I'm so glad you came," Senator Morrison said. "Not many of my constituents come to the office." Ruth made a mental note that the senator looked just like the photo on his website—the closely cropped graying black hair, black framed glasses, and piercing blue eyes.

"I really like to keep in touch with what's on the mind of folks in the district," the senator said. Ed and Ruth nodded and smiled. All the while, Ed was thinking that the next election is six months away and the senator is looking for votes.

"What brings you here today?" the senator asked looking from Ed to Ruth, and then back to Ed. Wondering if Senator Morrison was trying to bond with Ed, "man to man," Ruth decided to let Ed answer. She knew that a person's learning style is an important component of understanding him.

She reminded herself that she was here to forge a relationship as well as to advocate for issues that the senator will soon be voting on. She made a strategic decision not to let her anger about the times her two older brothers jumped in to answer questions that were directed to her interfere with this meeting.

Ed described the major role the shelter played in families' lives and the importance of keeping enough funding for this vital safety net. Ed gave an example of a mother with two children, ages three and five, who stayed at the shelter for eight months.

The woman was laid off from her job as a stocking clerk at a big box store where she had worked for two years at just above the minimum wage. With less income, she couldn't keep up with her rent. Although sympathetic to her plight, her landlord needed her rent to pay his mortgage on the two-family house.

The woman had hoped to stay with her mother for a few months until she found another job. But her mother lived in a one-bedroom apartment in senior housing. When the management discovered that her daughter and grandchildren were living there too, the mother was told they had to leave or she would be evicted. If not for the shelter where Ed and Ruth volunteered, Ed explained, this woman and her children would be on the street.

After Senator Morrison nodded his head in agreement and looked at her, Ruth jumped in with how important and cost effective preventing homelessness can be. She cited a state-funded program Sue had told her about that gives families emergency funds for back rent and overdue utility payments if this money can help them stay in their dwelling.

Such a fund might have helped the mother in this example remain in her apartment until she was employed again. The problem, Ruth emphasized, is that the program's funds were depleted in four months because the need was so great. For the rest of the year, applicants had to be turned away.

"I'm on your side about the importance of the program," the senator said. "But in these tough financial times, I'm not sure we can afford to fund every worthwhile program."

As Ruth nodded in agreement, Ed went on to say, "We know that money is always a concern, especially for someone in your position who has the tough task

> **Understand and acknowledge mixed feelings.**

of having to balance a far too small budget. We can understand that."

"But we are convinced that the government has a responsibility to help people in dire straits. Many of our friends and neighbors tell us they feel the

> **Describe the issue in a different way to reflect your beliefs.**

same way. So do many people in our church," Ruth said.

Ed thanked the senator for his compassion, remembering the importance of expressing appreciation to a lawmaker.

> **Express appreciation to your lawmaker.**

During the discussion, Ed decided he would ask two or three like-minded constituents he knew to email, write, or phone Senator Morrison and strongly encourage him to prioritize voting for adequate funding for homeless shelters and for homeless prevention programs.

Ed wondered whether he should ask Senator Morrison if he would like to have a district meeting about family homelessness with a few other constituents. Ed thought that since the senator was up for re-election soon, he might jump at the chance.

When Ed suggested such a meeting, Senator Morrison leaned forward, smiled, extended his arms

> **Form a small group of like-minded people in your lawmaker's district.**

on his desk and said, "I'd love to." Ed told the senator that he and Ruth would arrange something soon and coordinate the date with his aide. Ed and Ruth thanked the senator and said they would look forward to seeing him at the meeting in the district.

Walking down the corridor away from Senator Morrison's office, Ed and Ruth grinned at each other. Both were eager to report back to Sue about their first ever meeting with an elected official.

John

John is a 31-year-old computer consultant. Some of his clients are social agencies that send homemakers to help poor, frail elders with shopping and laundry. These services make it possible for them to continue to live in their own homes, instead of in a nursing home.

John frequently sees flyers on the agencies' bulletin boards decrying funding cuts that cause service cutbacks to "vulnerable elders," as the organization refers to its clientele. He is particularly interested in the issue because his grandmother, now 83, always stresses she "wants to die in her own house, and not in one of those institutions."

A few years ago, after her hip replacement, Granny needed some assistance at home. Luckily, John's mother was nearby to help out. She bought Granny's groceries and washed her laundry.

What if Granny had to depend on a homemaker and the program couldn't add any more clients, John began to wonder. After emigrating from Italy to the United States as a young bride in the early 1950s, Granny spent over thirty years working as a factory stitcher to support her three children. She had never been able to save much money.

The flyers John reads shout, "Contact your lawmakers. Ask them to reverse the funding cuts for homecare." John has never spoken to a lawmaker and doesn't even have a clue who his state lawmakers are. He remembers a few postcards that turned up in his mailbox before the last election. They featured photos of candidates and asked for his vote. Usually, he tossed the postcards into the trash.

Even if John knew his lawmakers' names, how would he reach them, and more importantly, what would he say? "Politics isn't for me," he thinks. "I just want help to be available for people like Granny."

John's Story

Whenever John saw the yellow flyer shouting, "Contact your lawmakers. Ask them to reverse the funding cuts for homecare," he promised himself that he would get in touch with his lawmakers. But he "never got around to it." Still, he was very aware that the real reason he put this off was his discomfort. Would he be asked questions he couldn't answer? Would anyone care about his opinions?

Feeling increasingly guilty, one day John took a closer look at the flyer. It mentioned that people could phone, write, or email their lawmakers. When John read the word "email" he felt a wave of relief.

"How could I have overlooked that easier and less personal way to tell them what I think," John said to himself, "especially because I am a computer consultant."

He also noticed that the flyer mentioned how people can learn who their lawmakers are. He could get that information from a website, call his city or town hall, or phone the state capitol.

John's Email

His personalized emails to his state representative and senator began with his thoughts as a grandson:

> **Register your opinion.**

> *From personal experience, I know how much having a homemaker can help an elderly person stay in her own home rather than move to a nursing home. After my grandmother's hip replacement, she needed help with showering, doing laundry, and grocery shopping. Luckily, her daughter, my mother, lived nearby and could help.*

> *Otherwise, my grandmother would have needed a homemaker. If none was available because of funding cuts, she would have had to go to a nursing home—at a much greater cost.*

> *I urge you to reverse the funding cuts for homecare so that low-income elders who need*

assistance can get the help they need to remain at home and keep their independence.

The Responses

Within two weeks, John received email replies from both his state senator and representative. The messages thanked him for contacting them about the important issue.

His state representative said that he would work hard to restore funding for homecare services, that he had always been a strong supporter of the program.

His senator said that while she appreciated the important role homecare services played in the lives of elders, there were many competing budget demands. She would have to weigh them all.

While this was not the response John had hoped for, at least he felt good that he had registered his opinion, that he had shown his state lawmakers that one of their constituents was very concerned about adequate funding for homecare. He wondered if others in his district had contacted this state senator. Maybe he could ask his neighbor to email too. John decided that the next time he saw a flyer about an issue he cared about, he could again send an email.

Barbara and Maria

Ever since she could remember, Barbara's heart went out to people who were "slow," the term her best friend in elementary school, Maria, used to refer to her brother who had a developmental disability. Jimmy was an uncoordinated but friendly boy three years older than Maria. He attended a special class at their school. Maria made sure he remembered to take his lunch box home and held his hand when they crossed the street.

Barbara came to love Jimmy and appreciated his helpful ways. In October, every day after school, Jimmy asked if he could help rake the leaves that blanketed her family's lawn.

After high school, Barbara became a dental hygienist and Maria became a social worker. Jimmy and his family had hoped that he would be able to work at a sheltered workshop, run by a non-profit organization. The workshop offered people with abilities like Jimmy's employment and the feeling that they were contributing to the society.

When Jimmy was 23 and no longer eligible for public school, funds in the state budget for sheltered workshops were slashed. New applicants were turned away. Unable to function in a mainstream job, Jimmy now spends his days at home watching TV and getting increasingly depressed and withdrawn.

Whenever Maria sees Jimmy like this, she promises herself she will do something to get him the services he needs. Maria and Barbara often talk about how they would like to help Jimmy but neither knows what to do. The sheltered workshop had mentioned that the state cut their funds. Maria and Barbara wish they could tell the folks at the state house how cuts were affecting Jimmy.

But they are afraid they might be seen as troublemakers. Besides, they don't know whom to call. They are vague about who their state house lawmakers are or how to find out. Perhaps most of all, they are nervous about what they would say. "The folks at the state house know so much," Marie said to Barbara. "Why would they want to hear from either of us?"

Barbara's and Maria's Story

The last straw that spurred Barbara to action was when Jimmy told her, with tears streaming down his cheeks, that he knew he was a failure in life. Barbara's brown eyes teared up too, seeing the 24-year-old man she'd known since he was eight, so discouraged. She knew that his developmental disability meant he would never be able to hold down a regular job, even as a bagger in a supermarket. He needed a setting like a sheltered workshop where he could get the support and advice he needed from a kind, understanding supervisor.

Barbara vowed at that moment to take action to give Jimmy some hope. "If sheltered workshops in this area have to turn people away because of funding cuts, at least people should know what happens to those who are turned away," she said to Jimmy.

"I'm going to do something about it." Jimmy smiled at his long time friend and protector.

| **Describe issues in another way.** |

Their Letters

Barbara persuaded Maria to be part of the effort. They started by phoning the director of the sheltered workshop that didn't have room for Jimmy. "What can we do?" they asked the director. She suggested they tell their state house lawmakers what the budget cuts mean for Jimmy.

Energized, Barbara and Maria each wrote a letter to their state senator and representative, highlighting Jimmy's story. They also

> **Write a letter to your lawmaker and to your local newspaper.**

decided to write a letter to the editor of their local weekly newspaper to show people what the budget cuts meant for Jimmy and for others who needed a sheltered workshop.

When their letter was published, they sent a copy to their lawmakers with the message—we are sending you this letter in case you missed it in the newspaper. To their surprise, three of Barbara's neighbors told her they had read the letter in the newspaper.

The director of special education in the town's school department phoned her to thank her for the letter. He said he was very troubled by the sheltered workshop's funding cuts. He told Barbara that he too would write a letter to their lawmakers and to the newspaper.

The Responses

Soon, Barbara and Maria received thank-you notes from their state senator and representative. Both lawmakers said that Jimmy's story was sad and gave them a better sense of the hardships the budget cuts caused. While neither made a promise to restore funding for sheltered workshops, both did say that they would pay special attention to issues that affected people with developmental disabilities.

Barbara, Maria, and Jimmy all felt they had taken significant steps to highlight an important issue.

Evelyn

Evelyn and her eight-year-old son Bill have been receiving public assistance, sometimes called welfare, for the past two years. Evelyn, a single mother, lost her job as a restaurant cashier when Bill started having asthma attacks every few weeks. After four years on the job as a reliable worker, her boss reluctantly fired her because he could not depend on her to show up for work.

He was sympathetic to her plight of having to spend hours in the emergency room when Bill suffered a severe asthma attack. He also understood that Bill needed her at home afterwards. But the bottom line was that his restaurant required a cashier he could depend on.

Embarrassed that she is on public aid, Evelyn struggles to make ends meet on her twice-a-month check from the state. Several times, despite careful budgeting, she has fallen behind on her rent and electricity bill and was nearly evicted. She managed to stay in her apartment and avert becoming homeless only because a social service agency gave her money from their emergency fund for the back payments.

Evelyn knows that a housing subsidy would help stabilize their life but the waiting list for subsidies is closed. She impresses on Bill that being on public assistance is "their secret," and that he should not tell any of the kids at school, where he receives a free lunch.

Whenever Evelyn thinks Bill's asthma is under control and she can look for a job, he has another attack, requiring a trip to the emergency room and care at home afterwards. She plans to return to work full-time when Bill's asthma settles down.

One afternoon, Evelyn's neighbor stopped by her apartment with a flyer she spotted at her child's day care center. According to the flyer, state house lawmakers would soon be discussing how people on the housing subsidy waiting list, and those who couldn't make it onto the list, might get assistance. The flyer urged families to come to a hearing to tell their stories.

Evelyn hopes the housing subsidy list will be reopened. "I'd apply right away," she thinks. She doesn't realize that she can play an important role in advocating for more money to fund housing subsidies.

Evelyn's Story
Evelyn knew she would benefit from paying only one-third of her income for rent, the payment formula for someone

with a housing subsidy. Much better, she thought, than the 60 percent she now had to put aside for rent every month.

But when her neighbor urged Evelyn to accompany her and some friends to a state house hearing, Evelyn backed off. She was not "an activist" she told her friend, and couldn't see joining a crowd that was advocating for anything. "Besides," she said, "I'm busy taking care of Bill now that he's had another asthma attack."

Her friend identified with Evelyn's discomfort since she had felt the same way until four years ago. At that time, she attended a state house hearing about raising the minimum wage. She had been impressed with the stories people shared with the panel of lawmakers hearing testimony. Many who told their stories worked long hours at minimum wage, or held two minimum wage jobs, just to make ends meet.

"I understand if you don't want to come to the state house hearing," Evelyn's neighbor said. "But at least phone our state senator to ask her to increase the number of housing subsidies. Tell her how much it would help you." The neighbor gave Evelyn the senator's phone number. "It'll just take a couple of minutes. The senator's aide will answer and won't ask you a lot of questions. Make sure to say you live in the senator's district."

"I'll see," Evelyn said. "I have to get my laundry out of the dryer now," and turned away.

The Phone Call

Evelyn couldn't stop thinking about making the phone call. The next day, Evelyn punched in the number her neighbor had given her, even though her palms were sweating and her stomach was contracting. She wasn't prepared for the friendly voice that answered saying, "This is Senator Holt's office; may I help you?"

"I live in the senator's district," Evelyn began. She hoped the person on the other end of the line wouldn't notice the catch in her voice. "I want to ask the senator to increase the number of housing subsidies. I am on welfare and spend 60 percent of my income for rent. If I had a housing subsidy, I would have more money to buy nutritious food for my eight- year-old son who has asthma."

"Thank you so much for calling," the aide responded and asked again for Evelyn's name and her address. "I will relay your message to the senator."

> **Share your firsthand experience.**

The Response

Three weeks later, Evelyn received a letter from Senator Holt saying that she appreciated her call and was very supportive of increasing housing subsidies.

CHAPTER 6

Adapt Your Everyday Interpersonal Skills to Influence Lawmakers

Abilities You May Take for Granted

Eleven Techniques to Use

- Register Your Opinion: Phone, Email, Write
- Build a Relationship With Your Lawmakers
- Get Acquainted With Your Lawmakers
- Understand Your Lawmakers
- Share Your Firsthand Experiences
- Stay Focused on Your Goals
- Express Appreciation to Your Lawmakers
- Express Disappointment to Your Lawmakers
- Describe Issues in Another Way
- Recognize and Acknowledge Mixed Feelings
- Form a Small Group of Like-minded People in Your Lawmaker's District

Register Your Opinion: Phone, Email, Write

Lawmakers pay close attention to communications from their constituents. A phone call, email, or letter is sure to be noticed.

The lawmaker's aide, not the lawmaker, almost always answers the phone. She will write down your message and pass it on to the lawmaker. Seldom will the aide ask the caller a question. On the rare occasion when this does happen, if you don't have the answer, you can feel comfortable replying that you will get the information and phone or email it to her. To find that information, contact one of the relevant organizations listed in the Appendix, *Guide to Resources to Help You Advocate*. Before you hang up, you may want to repeat your point. For example, if your issue is homelessness, you may want to reiterate that you hope the lawmaker will strongly support programs that can prevent family homelessness.

Registering your opinion with lawmakers can sometimes tip the balance. Here are two examples of two lawmakers' replies.

> *A church member from an affluent district who phoned his state representative heard this response. "The homelessness prevention program isn't high on my priority list. I haven't heard much about it from my constituents."*

Another state representative communicated through her aide that, "I've received emails from two people on that issue. I don't know much about the issue but I'm going to look into it."

* * * * * * * *

Build A Relationship With Your Lawmakers

Everyone knows the importance of healthy relationships in getting along with people at home, at work, and in the community.

The same holds true for expressing opinions to legislators. Like everyone else, legislators feel more comfortable with people who listen to their ideas, whether or not they agree, and hear them out in a polite, friendly, and respectful way.

* * * * * * * *

Get Acquainted With Your Lawmakers

A general "get to know you" meeting with your lawmaker is a good idea and easy to arrange. Set up an appointment to meet at the person's state house office or during the regular office hours the lawmaker holds in your area. You may want to bring one or two other people with you for support. At the meeting, you might begin by saying that you are a constituent and haven't had a chance to get to know the person.

Surprisingly, few people stop by to see lawmakers during their local or district office hours. You are unlikely to have much competition for your lawmaker's attention. Check your local newspaper or phone the lawmaker's state house office for location and time.

You have experience getting to know people in your neighborhood, workplace, and other locales you frequent. Most people might not give much thought to the social skills used in these various settings. But the same skills apply in getting to know your lawmaker.

During the meeting, you might want to ask some of the questions listed in this chapter. Or, your lawmaker might take the lead. Play it by ear.

You may also want to invite your lawmakers or legislative aides to events such as a neighborhood block party or a crime-watch meeting. Community events like these offer informal opportunities for constituents to share their opinions.

* * * * * * * *

Understand Your Lawmakers

Boston City Councilor Maura Hennigan stepped in a pothole and broke her ankle while marching in a parade in her district. Soon afterwards, she called for a City Council hearing to investigate why the potholes weren't fixed before the parade, and why it took so long for the ambulance to arrive.

"It's a little embarrassing," The Boston Globe quoted her as saying, "when you're marching along in the parade, then you're laying on the ground."

What an excellent example of how a personal experience shifted to a political issue! Notice as you read this section, the ways a lawmaker's personal experience can shape his or her ideas and actions.

When you try to get a full picture of your legislator both as a person and as a political being, it's important to pay close attention to her words and body language. In a face-to-face meeting with a lawmaker, you can gather a great deal of information to help you better understand the person you are hoping to inform and influence. Pay special attention to the information the person shares, and what she is leaving out or seems reluctant to talk about. Notice her tone of voice and any hesitancy in her speech.

Some Questions You Might Want to <u>Ask</u> Your Lawmakers

What is your position on _____? (Fill in the issues you are concerned about). Lawmakers expect to be asked about their positions and usually welcome a chance to explain their points of view.

Advocacy Tip:
Some of this information is available in local newspapers, from people in your community, or from social service agencies. It is useful to know someone's position before a meeting, but not necessary.

Keep in Mind:
Has the lawmaker held this position for a long time or recently shifted his views?

If his position is relatively new, it would be helpful to know what affected his decision. Such information might indicate factors that sometimes influence him. While it would not be appropriate to ask the lawmaker whether his position has changed, he might give you a clue that you could follow-up. For example, if the lawmaker says, "I used to believe differently," you could ask, "What made you change your mind?"

Why Lawmakers Might Change Their Positions
- Research or survey report
- Calls or emails from constituents
- Conversations or calls from people he trusts or relies on such as friends, relatives, neighbors
- Conversations with other lawmakers
- Legislative debates
- Pressure from legislative leaders
- Television report or newspaper article

More Questions to <u>Ask</u> Your Lawmakers
- What are your priorities in the legislature?
- What committees are you on?

- What made you want to become a lawmaker?
- What kind of work did you do before you became a lawmaker?

Some Questions You Might Want to Keep in Mind, But Not Ask During a Meeting

- How have the lawmaker's personal experiences, or those of his family or friends, affected his positions?
- Does he want to become a leader at the state house?
- Does he think that raising important issues is part of his role?
- How receptive is the lawmaker to others' opinions? And to whose opinions?
- What kind of learner is the person? Does he prefer examples and personal experiences, or is he swayed more by statistics?
- What is the lawmaker's background and how has it influenced his view of the world?
- Was his family affluent or did they struggle economically?
- Did he serve in local government previously?
- Has he lived in the district a long time?
- What kinds of jobs do his family members hold?
- What is his political party?
- Is he from a politically well-connected family?
- What is his religion, if any? Is religion important to him?
- What is his ethnicity? Race?
- Are his family immigrants or have they lived in the U.S. for generations?
- What is the person's family situation? Do any family members use services funded by the state, suffer

from the unavailability of services, or benefit from programs the state created?

* How does he explain poverty and its causes?
* Where does the lawmaker turn for information about issues? Specific newspapers, magazines, TV stations, websites, lobbyists, his legislative aide, advocates, constituents?

* * * * * * * *

Share Your Firsthand Experiences

Most lawmakers don't have the contacts that help them see for themselves how people's lives are touched by the votes they cast in the halls of power. Whether you live in poverty, have a disability, receive or need human services, have been homeless or at risk of homelessness, or know a formerly homeless person, you have unique information to share. If you work or volunteer in a social service agency, hospital or soup kitchen, raise money for social causes, you too have valuable information to share.

Mention the ways you have seen that services or programs have helped. Convey information about how services that are currently unavailable could have helped. You will be seen as a credible source. Never underestimate the power of this contribution.

I've often described an early experience as a clinical social worker to show how issues that seem unrelated are really interconnected.

One of the first families I visited as a social worker for a state child welfare agency involved a mother who had whipped her seven and eight-year-old sons with a stripped extension cord. She was reported to the agency for child abuse by the hospital emergency room where she had taken the boys for treatment. The case landed on my desk on a snowy afternoon. I started the home visit investigation by asking what happened.

Mrs. Sanders, holding her two-week-old baby on her lap, admitted she had hit the boys. When I asked why, her brown eyes filled with tears. "They wouldn't go to school," she said, wiping away her tears. "I knew that if they weren't in school, the truant officer would eventually come to take them away from me." She said her 15-year-old daughter was now in a home for girls since she had refused to attend school too. "I don't want to lose the boys too."

"Why didn't they want to go to school?" I asked.

"I can't stretch my public assistance check far enough to buy them boots," she said, "and their shoes have holes in them. The other kids will make fun of them, so they won't go to school."

After I share this story with lawmakers or their aides, they are much more aware of the need to raise public assistance grants and to continue an annual clothing allowance.

In another story, a mother gives firsthand evidence that emergency funds to tide over her financially distressed family would have kept them from becoming homeless. As no one else can, she describes her family's plight when her husband was laid off from his job:

> "We were evicted from our apartment when my husband was laid off. He couldn't find another job, and we had used up our savings. We lived in a motel for 10 weeks until a room opened up in a homeless shelter, all paid for by the state emergency assistance program.
>
> "In the motel, we had no way to cook and no refrigerator. Every day, I filled our Styrofoam cooler with ice from the motel's ice machine so I could prevent the baby's formula from spoiling. I had wanted to nurse but couldn't because my own nutrition was so bad. My other children ended up malnourished.
>
> "If the state had given us just $2,500 to catch up on our rent, we would not have been evicted. Instead, they spent $100 a day to pay for the motel and then for our stay in the homeless shelter."

* * * * * * * *

Stay Focused on Your Goals

Every discussion with lawmakers should be directed towards your short or long-term goals.

Short-term goals might include:
- Establishing a relationship with your lawmaker
- Winning your lawmaker's vote for your issue
- Convincing a lawmaker to propose your issue as a priority in meetings with the leadership

Long-term goals might include:
- Maintaining a relationship with your lawmaker
- Engaging your lawmaker as an ongoing ally
- Being seen as a trusted expert resource, especially important if the lawmaker moves up to become a committee chair or to hold another leadership position

Avoid being drawn into a discussion about topics that are not on your priority list. For example, if your lawmaker says that she just came from a hearing about raising electricity rates, try not to become engaged in a discussion about utility rates. Listen politely but then shift the conversation back to the issues you are concerned about. You might say something like, "There are so many issues lawmakers have to deal with. I would like to talk about . . ." Then mention your issues.

* * * * * * * *

Express Appreciation to Your Lawmakers

Most constituents don't think of saying "thank you" to a lawmaker who voted the way they hoped she would. They assume that the lawmaker isn't interested in hearing from them or gets lots of feedback anyway.

Unfortunately, lawmakers seldom receive praise or thank-you messages from anyone. For this reason, every expression of appreciation makes an enormous impression. It's also important to remember that behavioral research shows that actions, which are acknowledged and praised, are more likely to be repeated.

As Director of Governmental Affairs for the National Association of Social Workers, Massachusetts Chapter, I advocated at the Massachusetts State House for adequate funding for many children's services. During a contentious budget debate, one state representative stood up before his colleagues to urge them to add $1 million to children's mental health services. His plea that children with mental health problems were being harmed by long waiting lists resulted in a near unanimous vote to add the funds to the budget for the coming year.

I happened to hear about the representative's impassioned speech from a colleague who watched the debate from the balcony of the House of Representatives. Although I was already one hour late leaving my office for dinner with my husband

and children, I decided to phone the representative's office to say how much I, and my organization, appreciated his speaking out on this issue.

"Thank you so much for calling," the representative's aide told me, stressing the "thank you." "You are the only one who called. It was a tough debate and a tough vote."

How do you know which issues are under consideration at the state capitol and in Congress? Check your daily and local weekly newspapers. Request to be on the email list of your senators and representatives as well as of organizations that advocate on issues you care about. You will receive timely information about actions that can further your cause. Refer to the list of groups in the Appendix, *Guide to Resources to Help You Advocate.*

* * * * * * * *

Express Disappointment to Your Lawmakers

Telling your lawmaker that you are disappointed or upset with his vote or statement lets the person know that you are keeping an eye on his actions. It also is a way to reiterate your interest in an issue.

An email, phone call, or letter with your message goes a long way. Most men and women don't communicate their displeasure to their lawmaker. Too often, they just grumble to themselves or to others who share their views.

Of course, it's important never to "burn your bridges." Words said or actions taken in anger or frustration would make future conversations impossible. Remember that even though you may strongly disagree with your lawmaker on some issues, you might be allies on others.

I have made phone calls and written emails or letters saying something like the following:

> *Dear Representative X: I was disappointed with your vote against adequate funding for the homeless prevention program. As a result, thousands of families will be denied money for back rent and overdue utility bills, money that could prevent them from becoming homeless. I hope you will reconsider in the future.*

* * * * * * * *

Describe Issues in Another Way

When issues are reframed, or seen and understood in a different way, it creates fresh ways of thinking. For example:

> *The change from the term "the handicapped" to "person with a disability" shifted thinking. "The handicapped" implies the disability is the most salient characteristic of a person who might be in a*

wheelchair. The term "person with a disability" calls attention to the person first, and then notes the disability. This wording encourages others to see the person's individual characteristics such as personality, sense of humor, job skills, and hair and eye color.

This reframing likely contributed to creation and passage of the Americans With Disabilities Act of 1990 that prohibits, under certain circumstances, discrimination based on disability.

Other examples of reframing are:

The change from referring to a child as "illegitimate" to "born out of wedlock" or "born to a single parent" shifted thinking. "Illegitimate" connotes there is something wrong with the child. "Out of wedlock" or "born to a single parent" describes the circumstances of a child's birth.

The change from referring to people as "dumb" (i.e., those who are not verbal) as in "deaf and dumb," to describing them as "mute" went a long way towards erasing perceptions that people who cannot speak are mentally deficient.

* * * * * * * *

Recognize and Acknowledge Mixed Feelings

Everyone, including lawmakers, feels ambivalent about some issues. Whether it's being of two minds about a topic or feeling pressure to decide which programs to shore up with more funding, and which to leave wanting, mixed feelings are part of the equation. Competing priorities can keep a lawmaker from sleeping well. For example:

A lawmaker might want to help prevent families from becoming homeless but think that the state can't afford more funds for a homeless prevention program.

A lawmaker might want to allocate additional monies so that children in foster homes can stay beyond the 18- year-old cut off. But she knows that if she doesn't vote for more school funding instead, the parents in her district will be up in arms.

A lawmaker might care deeply about protecting abused and neglected children but feel skeptical about proposed remedies, including parenting classes and increasing job training programs. Instead, she may lean toward immediately removing an abused or neglected child from the home and putting him in foster care.

Clues to mixed feelings are many. Sometimes your lawmaker might talk about her ambivalence. Other times, the lawmaker might communicate a similar position through words or body language. Or, she might disagree with your position.

To discover whether ambivalence might be playing a role, a constituent could say something like, "Some issues have lots of sides to them" or, "I wonder if there are aspects of what we are proposing that you might be able to support."

* * * * * * * *

Form a Small Group of Like-minded People in Your Lawmaker's District

---

Lawmakers are seldom invited to a discussion with other constituents who share your opinions about issues that are decided at the state house.

If you invite as few as two or three of these people to a meeting at someone's house in the district or in the lawmaker's local office, you will be seen as an important force. You might want to have regularly scheduled meetings, perhaps every few months. Then, just before relevant votes, members of your group could call, write, or email your lawmaker urging him to vote a certain way. For example:

> *Every few months, I hold a Friday morning meeting at my house with our state house representative and once in a while with our state senator. Attendance varies from two people to as many as eight. One*

Friday, as he was about to leave, our state representative said: "These face-to-face meetings in the district are the best."

Coordinated Phone Calls

A few phone calls from constituents on the same topic can have an enormous impact. This strategy is ideal for people who want to advocate for issues but have limited time. For example:

A few years ago, I asked two other social workers in my hometown if they would be willing to call our state senator about issues that affected low-income children whose families were receiving public assistance. When I heard from an advocacy group that one of our concerns was up for a vote, I phoned the others to alert them that now was an important time to call.

Later, when our senator actively supported those issues, I informed my two colleagues. Within a couple of days, the senator had three phone calls from constituents thanking him for his leadership on those issues. It was the first time he received so many calls.

CHAPTER 7

Letters to the Editor and Social Media

Valuable Communication Opportunities

"Dear Miriam: My letter made it into the Gloucester Daily Times today. Thanks for all your help. My neighbors were all excited that someone from the neighborhood finally wrote a letter. Maybe they will start to write their own. . . ."

These comments are from a mother of three who lives in public housing. She wrote her first letter to the editor after participating in an advocacy training that included a section on writing letters to the editor. Here is a part of her letter:

After reading the article, "Riverdale Park gets natural gas" (2/28/04), I was angry and disappointed. Not once in the article did I read a comment or opinion of anyone that lives in Riverdale Park. I had to laugh at the reference from the Gloucester Housing Authority, about improving the quality of our lives here, because now we constantly worry about how we are going to pay these huge gas bills. We did not have a choice when we were converted to natural gas. While being converted, Keyspan did not weatherize the houses as they promised and this housing is old and very drafty. I myself have an average bill of $160.00 a month. Last year I got by with a tank full of oil, which cost me $200.00 for the entire winter.

Why These Are Effective Communication Techniques

Letters to the Editor
The Letters to the Editor page is the most widely read section of print and online newspapers. Readers want to know what others in the community are thinking. Legislators scrutinize this section. Most weekly newspapers publish all letters that are submitted.

After your letter is published, mail a copy or its online link to your lawmaker with a note explaining that the letter details your views on the topic. This offers you another opportunity to communicate with your lawmaker. He is likely to send you a thank-you message.

Social Media Venues

Social media such as blogs relating to online articles, Facebook and LinkedIn entries, and Twitter offer opportunities to communicate your thoughts about issues. You can email a copy of your entry and/or send its link in a message to your lawmaker, with a note explaining that the entry describes your ideas. As with a letter to the editor, these venues offer additional opportunities to communicate your views to your lawmaker, who is likely to send you a thank-you message.

Ways to Use Letters to the Editor and Social Media Posts

- Introduce a new idea to readers.
- Remind readers about an issue that doesn't get much coverage in the media.
- Provide additional information about an issue.
- Highlight connections among issues.
- Offer another point or new perspective regarding an issue. Information not included in the article or editorial you are commenting on, or your personal viewpoint, is considered interesting, fresh information.
- Use the technique of reframing to shape an issue. For example, if an article or blog post complains about the tax "burden" but is silent about the many services that taxes pay for, you can point out the connection.
- Highlight inconsistencies in public policies.
- Praise the way a newspaper or a writer presented an issue.

- Point out that coverage of an issue was incomplete or incorrect. The letter can fill in the missing information or set the record straight.
- Thank a public official for a vote, or an action, or for speaking out. A letter or posting can also express disappointment about an official's vote or statement.
- Note an anniversary of an event. Use the opportunity to include information about an issue.
- Add a new voice to an issue, and draw fresh attention to it.
- Promote the work of an organization.
- Grab attention for your issue, and establish yourself as someone with a special viewpoint on the topic.

Tips for Writing Letters to the Editor and Social Media Entries

- Use a "news hook" to make your comment timely. That is, relate your statement to a news story, editorial or previous entry (if you are using social media).
- Try to keep your message under 300 words. Shorter is better.
- Use humor if possible.
- Make only one point per letter or entry.
- Use short sentences for easier reading.
- Speak from your own experience, if you can.
- If possible, suggest solutions to a problem.
- Try to appeal to readers' hearts as well as to their minds.
- Consider using disguised case examples to make your point. The human impact of an issue makes it more compelling.

For Letters to the Editor

Email your letter to the editor. Usually the Letters to the Editor page will list this information. If not, phone the paper for the editor's name & email. Paste your letter into the body of the email. Do not send the letter as an attachment. In the subject line of the email write, Submission: Letter to the Editor. Remember to include your name, address, phone number and email address, if you have one.

Or, FAX your letter. Get the FAX number from the Letters to the Editor page or phone the publication. Remember to include your name, address, phone number and email address, if you have one.

Or, mail the letter to: Editor, Letters to the Editor, name and address of the paper. Find the information on the Letters to the Editor page. Remember to include your name, address, phone number and email address, if you have one.

Phone the editor of the Letters to the Editor page two or three days after you email, mail, or FAX your letter to inquire if it arrived. Often letters get misplaced. Your phone call will help direct attention to your letter.

Send your letters to the major daily newspapers in your area but don't overlook your local weekly paper as a place to publish.

Don't give up if your first letter isn't printed. If you send enough letters over time, you are sure to see some published.

For Social Media Venues
Type your entry in the designated location.
Email the link or a copy of your entry to your lawmakers.

Effective Letters to the Editor: Examples

These examples are also effective as blog posts, Facebook, LinkedIn or other social media writings.

How we color the immigration issue

How revealing is this apparent slip of the reporter's pen, in the article "Immigration debate intensifies across state": "In Milford, where at least 1 in 10 is now foreign-born in an otherwise overwhelmingly white city, the impact of the recent immigrants has spurred new measures to deter undocumented immigrants from moving there."

To the reporter foreign-born equals non-white. But I grew up in Milford, in the 1940s and '50s, at a time when far more than 1 in 10 were foreign-born. Italians, Irish, Portuguese and East-European Jews– thick accents made up what seemed then a major slice of my parents' generation and the generation before. They were foreign-born but classified as "white" and considered family.

Times have changed. Now the foreign-born are assumed to be non-white. Is that why being foreign-born was so colorful and positive then, but so threatening and negative now? (Boston Globe 7/8/06)

I Am a Widow

I am a widow with two teenage children who has worked as a machine operator for 18 years at the minimum wage. An increase would give all low-wage workers and me the opportunity to better provide for our families and keep up with the cost of living. (Boston Globe 5/30/06)

Clueless crossword

Although this is perhaps not the most pressing issue of the day, Saturday's crossword showed how far we still have to go in terms of awareness of other cultures and religions. The answer to the clue "Hindu sect member" was "Sikh." Sikhs are not members of a Hindu sect, any more than Christians are members of a Jewish sect (the relationships are similar).

Sikhism is a monotheistic and egalitarian religious tradition, with approximately 23 million to 25 million adherents around the world, placing it ninth among world religions.

Yet, since Sept. 11, 2001, Sikhs have regularly been misidentified as Muslim, and have suffered from violence and harassment like Muslims. Identifying them as Hindus is no better.

Education is the key to understanding the many ways of being religious, whether here or in other parts of the world. Given the current world situation, this understanding is more crucial than ever for everyone, religious or not. (Boston Globe 8/27/08)

Support for RAFT

We read with great interest the article which appeared in the April 9 edition of The Beacon that highlighted the increased demand for social services experienced by faith communities in the Acton-Boxborough area. We commend the editors for presenting this important and timely information.

We would like to bring a related topic to your readers' attention, the Residential Assistance for Families in Transition (RAFT), a state-funded program that reduces homelessness by providing up to $3,000 in flexible funds to allow families to remain in their homes.

The decision about continuing funding of RAFT will come before the legislature and senate in the next several weeks. Level funding of RAFT is critical this year as the number of homeless continues to grow. This program will reduce the risk of homelessness for numerous low-income families and will ultimately save money for the citizens of Massachusetts by keeping these families in their homes and out of shelters.

In these difficult economic times we need to support this program and we encourage citizens to contact their state representatives to support continued funding for RAFT. (Acton Beacon 4/15/09)

Two of the Author's Letters to the Editor

Hightower's Hope

Jim Hightower's hopeful article ("What One Person Can Do," February issue) would have been even more encouraging if he publicized how powerful constituent voices can be, especially at state houses, and how little time that strategy can take.

Most people don't realize that just a few phone calls or emails make a difference. Five or ten communications often seem like a huge community interest in a topic. Why? Because most residents don't relay their opinions to their elected officials. During my time as an advocate and lobbyist for low-income and immigrant issues, I heard numerous lawmakers explain that at times one or two phone calls made a difference for them and their colleagues.

Such small numbers might not influence "hot button" issues like tax increases, funding for wars, or marriage equality, but they certainly play a role in funding for homeless prevention programs, housing subsidies, classes in learning English, job training, and other lifeline programs.

Lawmakers need to hear from their constituents. (Progressive Magazine, February 2010)

Visit Arizona at your own risk

I had better visit Arizona before the immigration law goes into effect, or I'll have to carry my birth certificate proving that I am a U.S. citizen ("Ariz.

governor signs tough immigration bill"). I surely won't want to bring my daughter-in-law, a naturalized U.S. citizen from Peru. I wouldn't want her to suffer the indignity of being questioned by police about her immigration status, and then being arrested if she forgot to take her naturalization papers. I wouldn't want my grandchildren—U.S. citizens—to see their mother taken away for no offense other than having dark brown eyes, brown hair, and a Spanish accent.

I wouldn't want to bring my U.S.-born daughter either, as she has her Jewish grandfather's olive skin and jet-black hair. Many years ago, her grandfather was subjected to racial profiling. As he rode a bus to his Southern California home from a day trip to Mexico, an immigration officer questioned passengers who looked Hispanic to him. "Where were you born?" the officer demanded. "Brooklyn, New York," Grandpa answered in his Brooklyn accent.

I'm glad that my mother, a 1938 refugee from Nazi Germany, isn't interested in an Arizona vacation. But then, her skin is lighter, and she speaks English with a German accent. I guess she would be safe from suspicion, at least for now. (Boston Globe, 4/27/10)

CHAPTER 8

The Extra Power of Specific Groups

A Special Advantage, A Special Responsibility

Lawmakers and their aides consider individuals who are members of certain groups especially knowledgeable about the issues for which they are advocating. These people's extra power and credibility comes from their unique or firsthand experience.

Some are living with the situation or problem; others may work closely with people experiencing the difficulty. For some, their faith or conscience propels them to speak out against an injustice. These individuals are often seen as witnesses to what is happening to people and to the environment. All are constituents as well. Examples in this chapter depict real life and likely situations.

This chapter takes a close look at why these people are in a distinct position to play a critical role in reducing the root causes of harmful conditions. Many readers will discover that they are members of several groups that have additional power when they share their views with lawmakers.

It is also important for people in these groups to encourage those they know who struggle with difficult issues to share their stories. Hearing firsthand from individuals who experience a hardship, or have overcome one with the assistance of services or programs, can make an indelible impression on lawmakers.

The Power of Volunteers

Joan
Once a month Joan, a grandmother of four, buys an extra box of spaghetti and drops it in the carton marked "Donation for the Food Pantry" inside the supermarket's exit door. She feels good about having a role in "helping the hungry," as she puts it.

Joan doesn't realize that she could take another powerful step to help. She could call or write her lawmakers with the simple message, "I donate food to the food pantry. I urge you to put helping hungry people at the top of your agenda." Lawmakers need to hear Joan's powerful message.

Diane

Diane, a single woman in her 30s, expresses her concern for homeless children by playing with pre-schoolers at a homeless shelter two hours every week. In the training for her volunteer work, Diane was shocked to learn that one-third of mothers who are homeless hold down a job but don't earn enough to afford an apartment. A rent subsidy would have helped many of them pay rent and avoid homelessness. Unfortunately, the waiting list for the subsidy program is several years long. Diane could urge her lawmakers to allocate more funds to the program and share her observations. Lawmakers need to hear her powerful message.

Individuals who volunteer make a loud statement. "I care enough to donate my time to help others." Volunteers who perform "hands-on" work can be found in scores of settings, from social service agencies, homeless programs, hospitals, schools, and neighborhood groups, to recycling programs and park cleanups.

With so many people strapped for time, volunteers win particular respect. Lawmakers understand that volunteers have firsthand experience with tough situations and know what they are talking about. Volunteers have the added advantage of describing difficult situations without others wondering if they are speaking out for personal gain.

Volunteers need not be experts on policies or legislation. Their invaluable contribution lies in sharing their concerns with lawmakers, and asking them to prioritize solving the underlying problems that cause the harmful conditions. A clear request from constituents encourages lawmakers to pay special attention to proposals that address concerns highlighted by residents of their district.

The Power of Members of Religious Congregations

Carl

Carl Miller of Trinitarian Congregational Church in Concord, MA, walked 20 miles annually for 32 years in a Massachusetts Walk for Hunger to raise money for food pantries frequented by hungry people. As chairman of his church's Social Concerns Committee, Carl was eager to focus on eliminating the underlying causes of family homelessness. With his leadership, the Social Concerns Committee sponsored the first interfaith forum on family homelessness in their suburban area.

Afterwards, Carl invited members of the Social Concerns Committee and representatives from nearby congregations to a brainstorming meeting. This group formed a steering committee and created a family homelessness advocacy network that sponsors an annual community awareness forum on family homelessness prevention. Usually attended by close to 150 people, the forum invites lawmakers, advocates, and formerly homeless parents to speak about the reasons families become homeless as well as the remedies lawmakers will be voting on.

Now called the Advocacy Network to End Family Homelessness, the group encourages voters to join their

Action Alert Network. Based on information from lead advocacy organizations in Massachusetts, the Advocacy Network Steering Committee selects several topics regarding homelessness prevention that are before the legislature. The Committee then shares information with Action Alert members and suggests the best time to communicate their opinions to lawmakers.

Many of the Network's members phone or email as a result of Action Alerts. They report how easy it was to register their opinion and how receptive the lawmaker, or his aide, was to their call.

In response, one representative wrote to Carl Miller saying she was adding additional funding for adult basic education and job skills training to her list of state budget priorities. At two recent forums, five lawmakers told the audience that Network members' letters, emails and calls have led them to adopt key Network programs as their priority issues.

Congregants in this advocacy network, as well as congregants everywhere, have a two-fold message to lawmakers. Those who volunteer can communicate observations from their volunteer experience. They can also join congregants who may not volunteer in stressing that the tenets of their religion call for helping the poor or protecting the environment. That argument makes sense to many lawmakers, whether or not they consider themselves religious. Lawmakers who are observant may be drawn in emotionally as well as intellectually. Lawmakers need to hear their powerful message.

The Power of Human Services Workers and Community Workers

Josh

Josh, a case manager at a home health agency, is in an excellent position to describe how having a home health aide makes it possible for an 89-year-old woman to continue living in her own home instead of moving to a nursing home, a far more costly alternative. The aide comes for four hours three times a week to help the woman with showering and shopping. Josh's information might convince his lawmaker to vote against funding cuts for home care. Lawmakers need to hear his powerful message.

Individuals who are employed in human services and community-based organizations are experts on how programs and polices affect real people and communities. Daily, they witness the ways services can help people of all ages, and how the lack of services creates hardships and displacements. Their observations can quickly put a face on policy issues. Lawmakers are eager to learn about the direct impact of the programs they vote to fund fully, to fund inadequately, or not fund at all.

Community workers are also in an excellent position to mobilize colleagues to share typical client stories with lawmakers. Many organizations encourage clients or consumers to tell lawmakers their own story.

The Power of Mental Health Professionals

Lisa

Lisa, a social worker, is employed by a community mental health center. Her clients are low-income people with psychiatric illnesses. Many have been hospitalized for their problems and depend on medication to help stabilize their lives.

Stability for everyone includes a reliable place to live at an affordable price. With a dearth of such apartments or rooming houses, Lisa's clients often find that housing instability adds to their psychiatric difficulties. Some are able to work at low-wage jobs. Others, unable to work regularly, receive Social Security Disability benefits. Too many end up living in homeless shelters. When Lisa asks lawmakers to allocate more funding for housing subsidies that can help people like her clients, she carries a powerful message lawmakers need to hear.

Wanting to do more, Lisa asked colleagues at a staff meeting to contact their own lawmakers about the urgent need for housing subsidies. Many said they were reticent to call, never having spoken with a public official. Lisa described her own call to her lawmaker.

"I was nervous," she said as her colleagues nodded in agreement. "To my relief, his aide answered. I just said I lived in the district and was calling to ask the representative to support more funding for housing subsidies. When I heard an 'uh huh' on the other end of the phone, I went on to say that as a social worker working with mentally ill people, I know that

many of my clients would be able to manage their own affairs better if they had a stable place to live. The aide thanked me for calling, said she would share my message with the representative, and asked for my address and phone number."

Psychologists, social workers, psychiatric nurses, and psychiatrists all have abundant evidence of how services can help and how their absence harms. Too often, these professionals share these concerns only with colleagues, and not with lawmakers who have the power to address the root causes.

The Power of Health Care Professionals

One Concerned Physician

A suburban physician signed up for an Advocacy Alert list that notified members when their state house lawmakers were considering legislation to prevent family homelessness, an issue that pulled at his heartstrings. When he received the email urging people to call their lawmakers, he decided he could help.

For the first time, he phoned his state senator and representative. He urged them to vote for more funds for the lifeline program that gave families money for back rent and utility bills if that would mean the difference between staying in their own home or becoming homeless.

"I felt so empowered," he wrote in an email to the coordinator of the Alert list. This physician has a powerful message that lawmakers need to hear.

Physicians, dentists, nurses, physical, occupational and speech therapists, along with other health care professionals have a wealth of information that can influence decisions made in the halls of power.

As with others who provide services, health care professionals have valuable insights about how seemingly separate issues are inexorably connected. A dentist can speak about the importance of insurance coverage for preventive dental care for very low-income people who receive Medicaid, the government's health insurance for the poor.

A pediatrician can point out that sufficient money for food is key to very low-income children growing and developing adequately. A physical therapist can describe how an elderly woman who is recovering from a stroke depends on Meals on Wheels, a partially state-funded home delivery service, to assure she has adequate nutrition.

A nurse can describe that a six-year-old homeless girl hospitalized with pneumonia who lives in a car with her mother will stay in the hospital longer than kids with permanent homes, driving up hospital costs. Wouldn't it be more economical to give the family a housing subsidy so they could afford an apartment, the nurse might ask, urging her lawmaker to vote for more adequate funding for rental vouchers.

The Power of Teachers and School Personnel

Judith

Judith is a special education teacher in a suburban community in which an increasing number of homeless children have entered the school system. The children and their families live in the community's motels when family shelters in cities are filled to capacity. From her firsthand experience, Judith knows the effects of homelessness on children and their parents. When she asks lawmakers to support homeless prevention programs, they understand that she knows what she is talking about. Judith has a powerful message that lawmakers need to hear.

Paula

Paula, a family and consumer sciences teacher in a small city high school, sees a number of teens who are homeless. Some live in homeless shelters. Others sleep on a couch at various friends' houses. Sometimes this happens when a mother of boys has to move to a family shelter that does not allow males older than 12. Other times, there isn't enough room at a friend or relative's home for all the children in the family. None of the teens want the other kids at school to know of their plight.

Paula protects the teens' privacy, and finds ways to help them. She unearths funds to pay for their $10 lab fees. She keeps extra t-shirts in her storage room for students who need a clean shirt. She knows they won't be able to do homework on the Internet since they rarely have access to a computer. They can't come before or after school to use the school's computers because they have to ride the special bus to the shelter, motel, or a friend's house.

Every day, Paula sees the toll homelessness takes. The youths fall behind in school. They have a high absentee rate. Some are quick to anger or become depressed and stop trying. They can't afford the rites of passage other students take for granted, including attending proms or getting a driver's license. Paula would be doing a real service to the children she struggles to assist if she shared her firsthand knowledge with her lawmakers. They need to hear her powerful message.

Teachers like Judith and Paula, principals, superintendents of schools, school committee members, and guidance counselors have enormous data about the effect of federal, state, and local policies and laws on students. Often, these educators speak up about funding for the schools, including for important and well-publicized purposes such as classroom size. Their firsthand knowledge about other issues, such as homelessness and drug rehabilitation programs, can make a significant contribution to the legislative debate.

No one has more credibility than a teacher speaking about the need for a breakfast program at a school with very low-income students. When families are unable to afford enough food for their children, the school breakfast becomes an important source of their daily nutrition. Teachers know all too well that hungry children have a harder time concentrating on learning.

Or, a principal could urge a lawmaker to support more environmental regulation by describing that the exhaust from a waste treatment plant is polluting the air around his school.

The Power of Parents

Parents know their children. They watch them grow, learn, and develop. Individually, or working together in organizations like parent-teacher groups, parents have enormous power to inform and persuade lawmakers. Parents of all income levels can tell lawmakers the importance of class size and exposure to teachers from different backgrounds, ethnicities and races to prepare students for the future. They can also highlight that children's learning is hindered if they don't have textbooks they can take home or if their classroom teacher does not have paper for students to do their written work.

The Power of People Directly Affected, Their Friends and Relatives

Countless individuals living with mental or physical disabilities, in poverty, with illness, or confronting other difficult life circumstances have a front row seat when it comes to seeing and experiencing the consequences of lawmakers' votes. So do their relatives, friends, neighbors, and co-workers. When any of these people communicate their thoughts and concerns to their lawmakers, the issues gain special attention in the halls of power.

Power of Low-Income People

Christina and Joe

Christina and Joe barely manage to make ends meet. Each works at a low-wage job. Joe is a gas station attendant. Christina is a teacher's assistant in a first-grade classroom in their city's public school system. Although they both struggled to finish high school, they are determined that their three children go to college so they can have a better life.

Their children, Tom, Jen, and Bill, ages ten, eight, and six respectively, enjoy school and the class parties where students are asked to bring a treat for all their classmates. But the family budget can't cover money for a two or three-dollar bag of candy or chips. To find extra money, Christina and Joe sometimes skip dinner for a few days, telling the kids that they aren't hungry or that they had a late lunch. They hope the kids won't catch on. Christina and Joe have a powerful message about the importance of raising the minimum wage that lawmakers need to hear.

Lower-income parents can share how much better their children learn when they don't have to worry about whether the family will be able to stretch its paycheck to cover both rent and fuel costs. Or, a parent can describe a child's concern about whether there will be enough money to pay for school supplies or a class field trip. Both situations make a strong argument for legislation to boost housing and fuel subsidies, raise the minimum wage, or institute a larger tax break for lower-income families.

People who struggle to make ends meet—or lose that battle—have invaluable information about the ways that laws and policies affect their lives and well-being. Such people have a unique credibility that others cannot replicate. Lawmakers usually listen intently to people's stories that reach their hearts as well as their minds.

Power of People With Disabilities

George

George, a 30-year-old college student who has spent most of his life in a wheelchair because of severe cerebral palsy, lives alone in a handicapped accessible apartment near the school. His personal care assistant, who comes four hours a day to help with bathing, dressing, laundry, cleaning, and meal preparation makes it possible for George to live independently. Without this state-funded service, he would be in a nursing home.

George has a powerful story to tell lawmakers when proposed budget cuts threaten to reduce funds for the personal care attendant program. George could also describe how curb cuts in disrepair make it difficult for him to maneuver his wheelchair to cross the street.

People with physical, developmental, or psychological disabilities can share their firsthand experiences about which services help them be as independent as possible, and the consequences when such services are not available. Their messages can give lawmakers a closer look at circumstances that might otherwise elude them.

The Power of Immigrants and Refugees

Diego and Ana

With his wife, eight-year-old son and five-year-old daughter, Diego immigrated to the U.S. for a better life. Back home in Peru, the couple barely earned enough to buy food. Diego sold cell phones and his wife, Ana, was an assistant teacher in a day care center.

Here in the U.S., because of their minimal English, they are restricted to low-income jobs. Diego works long hours stocking shelves in a supermarket while Ana cleans houses. Both study English from books in the little free time they have but are eager to attend formal classes.

However, there is a two-year waiting list for tuition-free classes. Diego and Ana hope to qualify for better paying jobs that would mean more time for their children and an apartment without roaches. But first their English needs to improve. Speaking better English would also enable them to communicate with their children's teachers.

Typical of the challenges many immigrants face, Diego and Ana's story can give lawmakers a clear lens on an immigrant experience.

APPENDIX
Guide to Resources
to Help You Advocate

Many national organizations have state and local chapters and legislative alert email listserves. They gladly add names of people who wish to receive information about current issues at critical times before votes. Below is a partial list of key organizations. Many national groups can direct you to local affiliates for information about issues and legislative debates in your state.

National Organizations
AARP
http://www.aarp.org

The Arc of the U.S. (formerly, the Association for Retarded Citizens)
http://www.thearc.org

Assessing the New Federalism, A Project of the Urban Institute
http://newfederalism.urban.org

Bread for the World: A Christian Voice for Ending Hunger
http://www.bread.org

Center for Community Change
http://www.communitychange.org

Center for Law and Social Policy
  http://www.clasp.org

Center on Budget and Policy Priorities
  http://www.cbpp.org

Center on Urban Poverty and Social Change
  http://povertycenter.cwru.edu

Children's Defense Fund
  http://www.childrensdefense.org

Coalition on Human Needs
  http://www.chn.org

Common Cause
  http://www.commoncause.org

Conservation Law Foundation
  http://www.clf.org

Food Research and Action Center
  http://www.frac.org

League of Conservation Voters
  http://lcv.org

League of Women Voters
  http://www.lwv.org

National Alliance on Mental Illness
  http://www.nami.org

National Association of Social Workers
  http://www.naswdc.org

National Center on Family Homelessness
http://www.familyhomelessness.org

National Coalition for the Homeless
http://www.nationalhomeless.org

National Council of La Raza
http://www.nclr.org

National Campaign for Jobs and Income Support
http://www.commondreams.org

National Council of Jewish Women
http://www.ncjw.org

National Low-Income Housing Coalition
http://www.nlihc.org

Natural Resources Defense Council
http://www.nrdc.org

NETWORK: a National Catholic Social Justice Lobby
http://networklobby.org

Religious Action Center of Reform Judaism
http://www.rac.org

Stand for Children
http://www.stand.org

The OpEd Project
http://www.theopedproject.org

GLOSSARY OF TERMS

Advocacy: Activities that aim to influence public policy and budget allocation decisions within political, economic, and social systems and institutions.

Congress: The elected legislative body for the United States that holds the power to craft federal laws and budgets, and to repeal them.

Constituents: Residents of a lawmaker's district, whether or not they are registered to vote or are U.S. citizens.

Curb cuts: Ramps from a sidewalk to an adjoining street; curb cuts allow people who cannot easily use stairs (people in wheelchairs, with walkers, or pushing carriages) to move onto or off a sidewalk without difficulty.

Halls of Power: Legislative bodies such as Congress, state capitols, city or town halls.

Interpersonal Skills: Skills used to interact with others, sometimes referred to as "social skills" or "people skills."

Lawmaker: Another term for legislator.

Legislator: A person who makes laws especially for a political unit; a member of a legislative body.

Legislative Hearing: A panel of lawmakers who listen to oral testimony on topics under consideration in the legislative body. Submitting written testimony is acceptable too.

Legislative Leadership: Lawmakers in leadership positions in the halls of power.

Listserve: An electronic mailing list of people who have indicated they want to receive information from an organization or group.

Phone Bank: Organized telephoning of large numbers of people for a particular purpose.

Political Will: The readiness of lawmakers to take action on an issue.

Reframe: To describe or define issues in a different way.

Sheltered Workshop: A supportive work environment where people with disabilities are employed.

State Capitol: A building in which the state legislature meets.

State House: In some states, the state capitol is called the state house.

State Legislature: An elected legislative body in a state that holds the power to craft state laws and budgets, and to repeal them.

Testify at a State Capitol Committee Hearing: Share your opinions with a panel of lawmakers.

Ways and Means Committee: The committee in the legislature that deals with funding for bills and budgets.

ACKNOWLEDGEMENTS

My journey to complete this book would have been impossible without the encouragement, support, and patience—as well as assistance—of many people. I am grateful to them all.

Alice Chmielewski, my supervisor during my first year social work internship at Rhode Island Child Welfare Services, taught me the importance of focusing on people's strengths, no matter the plethora of their difficulties.

Violet Sieder, founder of the Massachusetts Human Services Coalition and my mentor in community organization and advocacy, generously coached me in growing the skills and confidence I needed when shifting from social work counseling to working for broader social change. This book is dedicated to her.

Elaine Brooks, a public relations and media expert, taught me about the key role the media plays in influencing public opinion. She graciously shared her expertise on ways to bring social justice ideas into the media arena.

Ginny Burns, chair of the political action committee of the National Association of Social Workers, Massachusetts Chapter, suggested that social workers could benefit from advocacy workshops. She developed some of the training curriculum for the workshops that I conduct and modeled effective teaching styles.

Carol Brill, executive director of the National Association of Social Workers, Massachusetts Chapter, granted me the freedom to advocate with lawmakers, work with the media, and run advocacy training for social workers and human services workers.

Claire Kashuck, executive director of the interfaith Cooperative Metropolitan Ministries, offered me opportunities to run advocacy workshops for religious congregations that were members of the organization.

Many social work and writer colleagues encouraged me— and urged me not to give up—when the task of writing this book felt insurmountable. In particular, Kathy Tully, my writing partner for several years, never wavered in her enthusiasm. "You've got to finish your book," I hear her insisting. An early reader of the material, Kathy's suggestions were always on the mark. Rae Simpson, another writing colleague, repeatedly said, "This is such an important book." Many of her suggestions are incorporated in the final version.

Other readers through the years are my friends Elaine Freedman and Jane Howard and fellow-writer Janet Cromer. I thank them for taking the time to read a draft, and for their perspectives.

Participants at my advocacy workshops—social workers, health care providers, immigrants, low-income community activists, and congregants—significantly influenced sections of this book. After they identified the techniques that helped them overcome their reticence to communicate with lawmakers, I allotted more time in the workshops, and in this book, to examples of conversations with lawmakers and their aides.

In a proposal writing class at Grub Street, a non-profit writing center in Boston, I learned both from the teacher, Stuart Horwitz, and from classmates that narratives would enliven my manuscript. Insightful members of a subsequent writing group—Amin Ahmad, Pam Giller, Lorna Kaufman, Bernice Lerner, and Tom Miller—were instrumental in facilitating my ability to take this route.

Members of my Social Justice Writers Group suggested useful additions to several chapters.

I am grateful to Pam Giller, my editor. Her patience and kind manner made working with her a pleasure, and the book easier to read.

John Amiard Oberteuffer did the layout for the book and its electronic versions. I thank him for his work, and his creativity.

I thank my daughter, Amelle, for the cover design and for her encouragement. I am grateful to my son Adam and his wife Esther for their support for the project, and to their children who were excited when they learned their grandmother was writing a book.

My undying thanks go to my husband, Will, who has always remained supportive of my social work activities and writing. He has been extremely generous with his time and graciously reviewed and proofread countless iterations of the manuscript. Whenever I considered giving up, he said with a gleam in his eye, "Remember why you began writing this book in the first place."

Without these people, this book would have remained an unfinished file on my computer.

Miriam Stein
Arlington, MA
January 2012

ABOUT THE AUTHOR

Miriam Stein, MSW, is a skilled advocacy trainer, consultant, speaker and writer committed to helping people from all walks of life who care deeply about social injustices become comfortable expressing their views to lawmakers.

Ms. Stein's extensive experience centers on state house lobbying and media work, as well as direct service in low-income communities. Her positions include: Director of Governmental Affairs at the National Association of Social Workers, MA Chapter; Director of Communications at the Massachusetts Immigrant and Refugee Advocacy Coalition; and adjunct instructor at schools of social work. Ms. Stein has been a featured expert on radio and TV news shows and in newspapers. A speaker at over 30 conferences, she leads eye-opening and enthusiastically received advocacy and media workshops. Currently, she is the advocacy consultant to the interfaith Advocacy Network to End Family Homelessness.

She was president of the Massachusetts Human Services Coalition, an organization of more than one hundred human services groups. She served on the Office of Justice and Peace Advisory Committee, Sisters of Saint Joseph, Boston, MA, the first non-Catholic and only member who was not a nun. She heads the Diversity Advisory Committee to the Superintendent of Schools in Arlington, MA and is co-chair of Arlington's Diversity Task Group.

Ms. Stein's awards include: Social Worker of the Year, National Association of Social Workers, MA Chapter; Martin Luther King Jr. Community Service Recognition Award; Citizen Award, Arlington Fair Housing Advisory Committee; and the Special Award, Foster Kids' Caucus of the Massachusetts Legislature.

Her articles have appeared in *Hadassah Magazine, The Christian Science Monitor, The Boston Globe, Boston METRO, thejewishwoman.org,* and others.

Ms. Stein is available for training, consulting and speaking.

Contact:
mstein@makeyourvoicematter.com
781-648-0255
www.makeyourvoicematter.com